A BODY
MADE
of
ALMOST

a poetry collection

by

ALEXIS DAKOTA

This is a work of creative nonfiction. Some names, details, and events have been changed for privacy or narrative purposes.

For inquiries, permissions, or bulk orders, please contact: alexisdakotawrites@gmail.com

ISBN: 979-8-99336504-0-1
First Edition, 2026
Cover and interior design by Alexis Dakota
Printed in the United States of America

for the girl I keep finding my way back to.

Contents

I — THE ACHE

longing · innocence · almost love

A Body Made of Almost

I am a body made of almosts—
of maybes and what-ifs,
of steps I didn't take
because I thought I needed permission to exist.

This is a body built from near misses
and not-quites.
Of hands that hovered,
of hollowed names,
of whispers I swear kept me warm through the nights.

A body stitched together
by sidelong glances
and phantom touches that never landed.

It remembers the nearlys,
the sudden hush before a touch,
the eyes that looked away too soon—
moments that lingered,
not quite memories, not quite enough,
but felt all the same.

They curled themselves into the folds of my skin,
left impressions without ever arriving in,
left warmth, then absence,
then questions with no mouths to answer them.

This body doesn't carry love

the way others do.
It carries the idea of it.
The shape.
The shadow.

It knows how to crave
without expectation,
to feel full
of nothing that ever stayed.

It has practiced the art of stillness,
of sitting pretty in silence,
of pretending not to want—
because wanting made the room go quiet.

I am a body made of almosts—
of might-have-beens and too-lates.
A soft architecture of what-if,
stitched together with threads of delay.

And it's not just the inexperience.
It's the shame of it.
The way people laugh
when you admit you've never been kissed.
The way they try to hide their pity
behind reassurances
that feel more like condolences.

It's not the kiss I mourn.
It's the years I spent pretending I didn't want it,
just to survive the silence.

But I did.
I still do.

And maybe that's the cruelest almost of all—
to spend your whole life learning to need less,
only to realize
you were always full of want.

But even that hunger
means you haven't given up.
Because wanting is a form of hope.
And hope,
even buried,
still grows.
So if all I've ever been is almost—
then let me be almost
and still becoming.

Let me be proof
that even a body built from ache
can learn to ask for more
and believe
it's not too late to receive it.

When Love Outgrows Its Innocence

Some girls had boyfriends by seventh grade.
Some kissed in basements,
touched hands in movie theaters,
got their hearts broken early and often—
learned what love looked like
when it was still clumsy and kind.

You never got the kind of love that still had milk teeth.
Soft. Untested.
The kind that bit but never broke skin.

There's a sweetness to love
before it knows any better—
when it still believes in its own myth.

It's the kind of love that giggles behind playground slides,
that laughs too loud,
that lets you want without shame.
That carries a curiosity
that doesn't yet know it should be afraid.

The kind of love that doesn't care
if your voice shakes
or your hands fumble
or your heart shows too easily.

But age strips that softness away.
By the time love finds you,

it's already learned how to guard itself.
It comes with exes, regrets, near-misses.
By the time it reaches you,
it's heavy with what came before.

Rules you didn't write.
Ghosts you didn't invite.

There's no chance to learn in secret anymore.
No room to fumble without consequence.
No space to mess up a kiss
and still feel giddy after.

You catch yourself wanting the kind of innocence
you only have before you know any better.
Not the childhood you lived—
but the softness of a first love
that didn't know how to bruise anything yet.

You didn't get that.
You came late to this world of affection and heartbreak,
and now it feels like you're trespassing.

You envy the memory of something
that was never yours—
that tender, naive spark
that belonged to those
who didn't yet know how bad it could hurt.

And still—
maybe there's some mercy in that.
Because you know what you're after now.
You know what was lost.
You know how precious that softness can be.

Maybe all you can do
is try to make a shade of it,
even now.

Hold someone with trembling hands.
Let yourself be unsteady.
Let yourself admit:
I don't know how this works.
But I'm here.

And maybe—if you're lucky—
you'll find someone who doesn't mind
that you showed up late.
Who doesn't care about the pages you missed.

Because the heart,
as worn as it might be,
still stutters the same
when it's touched just right.

And maybe,
if you're open,
you can still find a piece of that sweetness
you never got the first time.

Worth Without Witness

Some of us grew up without being chosen.
And maybe that's the blessing—
to know our worth
without needing a witness.

The Ones Who Weren't Kissed First

No one passed me notes in class.
No half-folded hearts, no nervous checkboxes
asking if I liked them too.

Love never knocked in homeroom.
I wasn't the girl they whispered about—
I was the one they dared each other to ask out.
A punchline. A placeholder.
A body they never meant to mean.

I was a bystander.
A witness to firsts that weren't mine.
Locker-side laughter,
fingers brushing in the dark of a basement party—
I memorized these moments
without ever touching them.

My first crush was a quiet thing.
So quiet I never told anyone.
So quiet it left no trace.
He looked through me
like fog on the bus window.
And I let him.

There's a peculiar silence that settles
when no one ever chooses you.
It doesn't howl—
it hums, low and constant,

a soft apology that attaches to your name.
I have no exes.
No stories about who hurt me first.
Only questions.

Only wonder at what it means
to be wanted without caveat.

So I loved from a distance—
archiving glances like heirlooms,
imagining the weight of a hand
that might rest on my thigh
without hesitation.

I told myself I was waiting for something real.
But sometimes I wonder
if real ever waits for girls like me.

Now, I flinch at attention
even as I ache for it.
Love feels like a room I don't know how to enter—
like it requires a password
I was never taught to say.

Still, I stand outside the door.
Still listen for footsteps.
Still hope it opens.

Even if it's late.
Even if I'm older now,
and innocence doesn't fit
the way it did on girls
who bloomed on time.

You Were the One Who Stayed

You thought it would happen by now.
That someone would've said it.
That they'd see you in the way you'd imagined—
face lit up like you were a secret worth telling.

You used to think love looked like movie theaters and slow dances,
like being picked first without having to ask.
But you were always just a beat off.
Too late to the rhythm.
Too early with your heart.

And while everyone else was out there
falling into other people,
you were quietly learning the shape of your own hands.
The way your voice sounds when no one's watching.
The way your stomach folds when you laugh too hard,
and how that, too, is worth keeping.

You weren't anyone's first.
Weren't scribbled in the margins of a boy's notebook.
Didn't kiss behind gymnasiums
or lose anything in the backseat of a car.

But you didn't stay untouched.
You were just touched by other things.
By silence.
By softness.
By the long road of becoming.

And god—
you didn't ask for it,
but you grew through it anyway.

You became the person who keeps showing up
even when no one else does.
Who knows how to sit with herself
without shrinking.
Who knows how to want more
without flinching.

You thought love was supposed to arrive
with someone else's hands.
But it came
when you stopped apologizing
for needing your own.

Waiting for the Joke

I am always waiting to be found out.
Like I slipped into a room I wasn't meant to be in.
Like I'm wearing someone else's skin,
and it doesn't quite fit right.

When they touch me,
I flinch—
not because I don't want it,
but because I'm bracing
for when they'll pull away.

Because that's how it started.

With dares.
With jokes.
With the way my name sounded
when someone else's mouth made it ugly.

The first time someone said they liked me,
it was a setup.
A punchline.
A game they played at recess,
a secret passed between snickers
while I stood there, red-faced,
pretending I hadn't heard.

And after that—
I learned.

That wanting was dangerous.
That being wanted was always a trick.
That desire came with strings
I wouldn't see until they yanked me off my feet.

So I stopped trusting it.
Stopped trusting myself in it.

I learned how to watch from the edges.
How to cheer for other people's love.
How to stay quiet about my own wanting
until it softened into something safer,
something small enough
to fold into my pocket.

And when someone did reach for me—
I was sure they were mistaken.
Sure I was the trick their eyes were playing.
Sure I was the dare they'd laugh about later.

So I flinch.
So I brace.
So I shrink.

I don't know how to stop thinking
that love is something I have to audition for.
That I have to shrink first,
or shine brighter,
or twist myself into a shape
that won't make them change their mind.

I have spent so long
watching from behind glass.
So long telling myself *later*.

After.
When I'm better.
When I'm less.

That now, even if someone reaches for me,
I don't know how to believe it.
I don't know how to believe
I am not some trick
their eyes are playing on them.

But I want to.

I want to know what it feels like
to stop auditioning.
To stop bracing.
To stop mistaking love for a test
I was never meant to pass.

I want to know what it feels like
to be wanted
without wondering
if I fooled them into it.

I want to know what it feels like
to stop shrinking.
To stop earning.
To stop waiting for the joke
to be on me.

I want to know what it feels like
to stand in the wanting
and not feel like I have to apologize for it.

To be looked at
and not search for the trick.

To be wanted
and finally, finally
believe it's real.

The One Who Made It Easy

I learned early
that it was easier to be the joke
if I told it first.
It landed softer, hurt less.

If I made them laugh,
they wouldn't look too long.
Wouldn't point too hard.
Wouldn't see what I was trying so badly to hide.

So I became what they wanted.
The loud one. The quick one.
The one who could spin the weight of things
into something light enough for everyone else to carry.

I learned to fill the air
before silence could turn dangerous.
To hand out stories like gifts—
each one wrapped in just enough sparkle
to keep them from seeing the parts of me
I was terrified they'd find.

If they were laughing,
they weren't looking too hard.
If they were laughing,
they weren't asking.
If they were laughing,
I could breathe.

So I kept them laughing.
I exaggerated just enough.
I was always a little louder than I felt.
I offered up the parts of myself
I didn't mind them picking apart,
so they wouldn't go looking
for the parts I did.

And god, I got so good at it.
So good at making it easy for them.
Easy to love at a distance.
Easy to keep around but not close.
Easy to laugh with
so they wouldn't have to ask
what I actually needed.

And somewhere along the way,
the act stopped being a choice.
It became the armor I forgot how to take off.
It became the skin I lived in.

I forgot how to stop doing it.
Forgot how to let the room go quiet
and believe I was still enough.

I want to know what it feels like
to be listened to
without having to earn it.
To be looked at
and not feel like I have to soften the gaze.
To be kept
without offering myself up first.

I want to know what it feels like

to be still
and be seen.
To stop being the one
who makes it easy—
and still be loved anyway.

Prayer Without a Name

There are days I pray without naming it.
To the coffee cup, to the cracked ceiling paint,
to the strangers who don't look away.

Everything feels like God
when you're desperate enough.

The Life I Live in My Head

In the life I live in my head,
I've been loved—
once, maybe more.
Softly. Entirely.

In that version,
they knew how to look at me
like I was the answer,
not the question.

It felt like warm hands on the sides of my face.
Like breath shared in the stillness.
Like knowing.
Not the kind you explain,
but the kind you carry in your spine.

In my head,
love arrived soft and certain.
It didn't flinch when I undressed my fear.
It didn't ask me to earn its staying.

We had arguments—
not about leaving,
but about which side of the bed was colder.
We had Sunday mornings and eye contact
and the kind of silence that feels full.

I made it all up,

but the ache is real.
My body mourns a closeness it's never had.
Grieves hands that never held it.

There's a ghost version of me somewhere,
well-loved and well-rested,
and she's lived a thousand lives
I can only write poems about.

But lately,
even the daydream stings.
Like I've rehearsed the feeling so many times
it's worn a groove in me
where the real thing should be.

So now I sit with the version of myself
who made all that love up.
Who built a whole life
from almosts and maybes.

I let her have her pages.
I let her write the softness she never got.

And when I close the book,
I don't call her foolish.
I don't call it a waste.

Some aches deserve to be named,
even if they never happened.
Some tenderness lives
just in the wanting.

And some of us have only ever been held
by the versions we imagine.

Just Outside the Warmth

Men are kind
when they want something.
I learned that the hard way.

I watched how the tone shifts,
how the smile softens,
how the world seems easier
for the ones they want.

I felt what it's like
to stand just outside of that.
To see the warmth that isn't meant for me.
To watch them bend over backwards
for the girls they want,
and barely lean in
for the ones they don't.

Some people don't see it.
They don't have to.
They've never felt the cold
of kindness that isn't offered.
Never carried the weight
of realizing
it was never about who you were—
only what you looked like.
What you could offer.
What they decided
you were worth.

I learned it standing beside the girls
who didn't have to try
to be wanted.
Learned it in the way their eyes
never stopped on me long enough
to mean anything.
In the way they spoke over me,
through me,
like I was air—
a gap between one want
and the next.

My friends never noticed the shift.
Never noticed how I stood
a little too still,
like maybe if I didn't move,
I could hold my place.
Never noticed how invisible I could feel
in a body that always took up space.

I learned to disappear
without leaving the room.
To laugh at the right moments.
To smile wide enough
that no one would see
how much it hurt.

I learned to pretend
I didn't see their eyes soften
for everyone but me.

And god—
the way it burns
when kindness isn't for you.

The way it hollows you out
when you realize
it was never about who you are.
Just what they see
when they look at you.

You learn to make peace with it.
To stop expecting softness.
To stop hoping to be seen.
To stop reaching for the warmth
that was never meant for you.

But the body remembers.
The body always remembers.

The Things I Never Practiced

There are things I was supposed to know by now—
how to let a hand settle on my knee
without every tendon turning to wire,
how to meet a gaze
and stay inside it.

I should have learned to move through closeness
the way others breathe:
unthought, unearned, theirs.

Kindness unsettles me.
I don't know where to store it,
don't trust what requires no payment.

I want closeness,
yet I wait for the moment it sends a bill.

Touch feels provisional—
a library book with a stamped-in deadline,
already ticking toward return.

So I hover at the threshold—
all pulse, no step—
examining hinges
instead of crossing the doorframe.

What I never practiced
has calcified into caution:

breath held at the edge of yes,
muscles braced
for a laugh I can't predict.

Still, want keeps its own hours.
It taps the glass at midnight,
asking whether the lock is stubborn
or whether I am.

Someday I'd like to reply
without translating every gesture into risk—
to receive nearness
the way a roof receives rain,
simple, unbargained for.

Until then I stay here,
learning the weight of my own hands,
testing the sound of welcome
in a mouth that has always
rehearsed for silence.

I Thought I'd Stumble Into It

I thought I'd stumble into it—
like finding a familiar face
in a crowd.
Like breath returning
after holding it too long.

Something quiet,
but certain.
A recognition before a name.
A pull in the chest
before the mind can catch up.

I thought it would unfold—
easy,
like soft fabric gathering in the lap.
I thought love would know where to place its hands,
would show up with open palms
and no agenda.

I thought I'd be ready—
that all the empty years
would make room for it.
That waiting would ripen me,
not wear me down.

But no one tells you
how waiting can turn into withering.
How longing, left too long,

starts to doubt itself.
How the heart rehearses so many firsts,
it forgets how to live them.
How hope can sour
when it's kept too long in the dark.

I don't know if I'm afraid of love
or of being seen in its light.
Of how small I might feel,
how much I might want.

I brace for sweetness
like it might shatter me—
and maybe it will.

But I stay open,
even when it stings.
Even when my body
doesn't know where to be held.
Even when I want to run
just as much as I want to be chosen.

I thought I'd stumble into it.
Maybe I still will.

But if I don't—
if it never comes easy—
let it still come honest.
Let it meet me where I am,
even if I'm trembling
when it does.

Chosen vs. Kept

What would it mean
to be chosen—
not *craved*,
but kept?

Warning Label

I don't know how to say I like you
without also saying I'm sorry.
Sorry for putting you in this position.
Sorry for noticing you first.
Sorry if it makes you uncomfortable.
Sorry if I got the math wrong—
if I mistook a glance
for something softer.

I don't have the kind of face
that gets to have harmless crushes.
When I like someone,
it feels like an inconvenience.
Like I should come with a warning—
this affection might not flatter you.

I try to keep it small.
A silent thing.
An almost.
A maybe.
A "just being friendly"
I never quite pull off.

But god
the way I rehearse casual laughter
like it might soften me
into someone you could see.
The way I avoid standing too close,

in case you think I'm expecting something back.

I get embarrassed just wanting.
Like I need permission
to look at you too long.
Like I've broken some rule
by daring to imagine myself
as someone you might want.

And the guilt?
It lives in my skin.
It whispers—
He doesn't know what you look like
with your clothes off.
He doesn't know
how much of you there is to hold.
He didn't sign up for this.

I wish I could like people
without feeling like I'm offering them a burden.
I wish I could want
without also apologizing for it.
I wish I could say I like you
and mean only that.

But most days, I tuck it away.
Behind polite smiles
and disappearing acts.
Behind jokes that leave just enough space
for you to pretend
you didn't hear what I meant.

And maybe one day,
I'll let the wanting be loud.
Let it live in my chest

without shame pressing down on it.

But for now,
it's a quiet ache.
A beautiful secret.
One I carry carefully—
so it doesn't spill
where it's not welcome.

The First Hands

The first hands that touched me like they meant it—
I felt my body stiffen
before they even finished reaching.

Heat blooming up my neck,
my heart so loud
I was sure they could hear it.

Their fingers brushed my skin,
and it was like my body wasn't mine anymore.
Like they'd found something in me
I didn't know how to offer.

I want this.
I've wanted this.
I've imagined it a thousand times—
the moment someone's hands would trace the shape of me
like I was worth remembering.

But no fantasy prepares you for the shock of it.
For the way skin burns under kindness.
For the way every inch of you tightens—
not because you want to pull away,
but because you don't know how to stay.

The first hands that touched me like they meant it—
they didn't have to press hard to leave marks.
Just a brush.

A graze.
A fingertip at the edge of my jaw.
That's all it took to undo me.

I thought I'd be ready.
I thought I'd open
like I'd always dreamed.
But I didn't.

I froze.
I trembled.
I held my breath—
terrified I'd ruin it.
Terrified they'd see
how unpracticed I was.
Terrified they'd stop.

The first hands that touched me like they meant it
were softer than I ever imagined.
And I didn't know if I wanted to cry
because it was finally happening,
or because I'd spent so long waiting
I wasn't sure how to let it in.

And god—how I wanted to let it in.
To melt beneath it.
To stop keeping score
of every way I've been overlooked.
To stop wondering if they'd change their mind
once they realized what they were holding.
To stop bracing
for the moment it would slip away.
To stop questioning
if I was too much, or not enough,
or both at once.

To stop living in my head
and finally, finally
feel it in my skin.

The first hands that touched me like they meant it—
I let them.
And maybe I trembled.
And maybe I didn't know what I was doing.
But I didn't run.
I stayed.

And that has to count
for something.

What It Means to Be Wanted

For so long, no one looked at you.

You watched the world fall in love with other people.
Watched hands slip into back pockets,
fingers trace over knuckles,
watched lips press into hairlines like it was instinct.

You watched it happen around you,
but never to you.

You were the friend.
The observer.
The one people called at midnight
to talk about someone else.

And you told yourself it didn't matter.
That love would find you when it was time.

But the years passed.
And it never did.

And so you waited.
For the moment it would be your turn.
For the night someone would touch your arm
like they couldn't help themselves.
For the morning someone would say your name
like it was something they missed in their sleep.

But love circled around you,
touched the edges of your life,
but never stepped inside.

You learned how to smile through stories
you would never have.
How to nod at advice you'd never need.
How to laugh at jokes
about things you had never experienced.

Then, one day, people started looking.

And you wanted to drink it in.
To let it fill you, stretch you,
make up for lost time.

To swallow it whole,
as if attention could reach the places
love never touched.

You let people want you.

Even if it wasn't the kind of wanting
that lasted past dawn.

Even if it was just a look across a bar,
a hand at the small of your back.

Even if it was fleeting,
shallow,
hollow.

Because what else was there?

You told yourself this was what you wanted.

To be seen.
To be craved.
To be beautiful, if nothing else.

But sometimes,
when the room was quiet,
you wondered if there was a difference
between being wanted
and being chosen.

If someone's hands on your hips
meant anything at all
if they never learned your middle name.

If the way they looked at you
meant more than the way they left you.
If being desired would ever be enough.

You spent years mistaking being seen
for being loved.
Mistaking heat for warmth.
Mistaking hunger for devotion.
Mistaking attention for something
you could hold onto.

But now —
you are learning the difference.

You no longer want hands
that only reach for you in the dark.
No longer want words
that only come easy over drinks.

You want softness.
Slowness.

Certainty.

You want someone who looks at you
like there is nothing to prove.

And maybe you don't have it yet.
Maybe you are still learning
what it means to stop settling for less.
Maybe you are still unbecoming
the person who thought she had to take
whatever she could get.

But you are getting closer.

Closer to the kind of love
that doesn't slip through your fingers.

Closer to the kind of love
that feels like coming home.
Closer to someone who will see you
and choose you—
every time.
And when they do,
you will know the difference.

Sometimes I think I want love.
Other times I think I just want an audience.
How would I even tell the difference?

Still Wanting Butterflies

They tell me to trust my gut now.
To listen for warning signs.
To read silences like red flags.

But I still want butterflies.
Still want the dizzy, stupid, teenage kind of wanting.
The flushed skin, the breathless maybe.

Not the calculated readiness of adult love.
Not the checklist.
Not the "what are we" talk
rehearsed in my head
three days too early.

I want the ache before the knowing.
The crush that ruins my appetite.
The smile I can't stop replaying
like a song I never get tired of.

I want to forget I've been hurt.
I want to want without proof.
To kiss without worrying who cares more.

I know better now.
I've read the signs.
I've memorized every rule of protection.

But still—

there's a part of me that misses
not knowing better.

That aches for innocence
like something I accidentally left behind
when I learned
how to be careful.

The Instinct Isn't Mine

I've never learned to trust my instincts.
Not in love.
Not when it matters.

They say you'll just know.
That the body leads.
That desire knows what to do
if you let it.

Like there's a choreography
built into the bones.

But mine never got the memo.
There's no inherited grace here.
No lineage of knowing smiles
or practiced touches.

Only guesswork.
Only hesitation
dressed up as composure.

I've spent years watching from the sidelines,
trying to pick up the rhythm
without ever being asked to dance.

I watched my friends learn it in real time—
awkward, electric, messy.
They got to practice.

They got to be bad at it first.

But when you're never chosen,
you don't get rehearsal.
You only get the pressure
to somehow be perfect
when the moment finally comes.

And so, I keep a script in my head.
Not of what I'll say,
but of how I'll look—
how I'll smile,
how I'll lower my voice
just enough to sound effortless.

It's armor disguised as readiness.
It's performance
disguised as instinct.

Because no one tells you
how heavy it is to carry want
without experience.

No one tells you
how sharp it feels
to want to be touched
and not know
if you can handle it.

Sometimes I fear that love will arrive
and I'll flinch so hard it won't stay.
That I'll be too rigid,
too late,
too behind.

But I don't need perfect.
I just need possible.

Something that doesn't rattle
when I reach for it.
Something that doesn't punish me
for not knowing how to begin.

If it comes,
I don't want fireworks.
I want room.
I want time.

I want to be allowed
to be new at it—
without apology,
without performance.

Let me misstep.
Let me forget the lines.
Let it still be mine anyway.

This Time, I Won't Pretend

I don't remember the first time
I swallowed a want whole.
But I know what it tasted like.

Like dust.
Like breath held too long.
Like the sound of someone walking away
before I'd decided to speak.

I learned early
that wanting without invitation
was the quickest way
to feel humiliated.

So I tucked my hunger
into quiet places—
between polite nods
and the kind of jokes
that keep things light.

Desire became a private ritual.
Like saying grace
for a meal that never came.

I told myself I was fine.
Told myself I didn't care.
Told myself
this body wasn't starving,

just disciplined.

But the truth is—
all the years I pretended I didn't want
just to survive the silence—
I did.
I do.
I want.

I want to be looked at
like I matter.
Not glanced at.
Not tolerated.
But seen.
Chosen.
Out loud.

I want a hand
that doesn't hesitate.
A voice that doesn't lower
when saying my name.
To be wanted
without secrecy
or pretext
or apology.

And it's not just about touch.
It's about presence.
About someone leaning in
instead of away.
About being remembered
when I'm not in the room.

I used to think longing
made me weak.

That if I wanted too much,
I'd ruin the little I had.

So I wore detachment
like perfume.
Something faint and convincing.
Something that made them think
I didn't notice
how invisible I'd become.

But I was always noticing.
Always watching other people get chosen
while I rehearsed being okay
with almost.

And now?
I'm done calling my hunger
dramatic.
Done dressing up loneliness
in "I'm just busy."
Done pretending
my skin doesn't shiver
when someone says my name
like it could mean something.

I want.
And this time,
I won't pretend otherwise.

Soft in Theory

They want me in theory.
In passing thoughts.
In 2 AM *what ifs.*

I'm the favorite tab left open,
message typed and never sent,
the secret they keep sweet and quiet.

They flirt like cowards—
all heat behind closed doors,
all silence when the lights come on.

They love the idea of me—
loud and clever,
soft in places they haven't earned
the right to touch.

But theory doesn't take you to dinner.
Theory doesn't introduce you to their friends.
Theory doesn't look me in the eye
and say I want this,
out loud,
where people can hear it.

I've been archived
in so many people's almost.
Tucked away like a guilty pleasure—
too much for the world,

but not enough to hold in it.

And I used to play along.
Used to be grateful
for the attention that almost
made it out of their mouths.
For the compliments
that came with disclaimers.
For the desire
that never made it to daylight.

But I am not a secret.
I am not a fantasy
to be folded up
and hidden in the glovebox
of someone else's shame.

I'm not the thing you want
only when no one is watching.

So unless you're ready
to say my name in public,
to hold my hand
without looking over your shoulder—
don't touch me in theory.
Don't want me in silence.
Don't come close
if you plan on leaving me in the dark.

Because I have spent too long
being almost
Being liked in whispers.
Being love you can't say out loud.

I want to be chosen.

In the kind of voice that carries.
In a room full of people.
Like I was never a maybe
to begin with.

I let them shelf me
under someday.

Under almost.
Under *just not right now.*
But I am not an idea.
I'm not some sweet distraction
you fold into your pocket
and pull out when it's safe.

I am flesh and feeling.
I am the kind of love
that deserves to be spoken out loud.

And I am done pretending
that a half-glance is enough.

If you want me,
want me where people can see.
Want me in sunlight.
In motion.
In the kind of way
that dares to stay.

Because I am not here
to haunt your fantasies.
I am not your secret.
And I am no longer flattered
by the ones who only want me
when no one else is looking.

When Love Was Loud

I miss when love was reckless enough
to be embarrassing.

When it showed up in Sharpie
on the backs of notebooks.
When it meant sweaty palms
and voices cracking in hallways.

When someone would say I like you
like it was the only thing worth saying.

I miss back when people
didn't know how to hide it.
They bragged. They blushed.
They shouted it too soon
and meant it anyway.

It was clumsy,
but it was honest.

Now—
love has learned
how to swallow itself.

It shrinks into half-phrases:
"yeah, we're talking,"
"it's nothing serious,"
"we'll see."

Like wanting too much
is something to be ashamed of.

And maybe that's why
I still crave the kind of love
that doesn't play it cool.

That doesn't ghost
to keep the upper hand.
That doesn't laugh
at its own sincerity.

I want the stupid kind.
The loud kind.
The kind that ruins your plans
because you couldn't stop
saying their name.

The kind that isn't afraid
to stand in front of everyone
and look foolish
for wanting.

Because what's the point of love
if it never lets itself
be seen?

II — THE HUNGER

conditioning · shame · compulsion

Hunger

I want to be chosen. I want to be needed. And I do not know the difference.
I have never known the difference.

Love, for me, has always felt like hunger—
something gnawing, something bottomless.
A stomach stretched too wide,
an appetite that does not subside.

I take what I am given
and tell myself it is enough,
that I am full,
that I can live off crumbs
if I just chew slow enough.

But the truth is:
I am always reaching.
I am always waiting for more.

I have called it love.
I have called it devotion.
I have called it patience.

But I think—*no, I know*—
it is hunger.

I have spent my whole life starving,
and I have mistaken every kind hand,
every fleeting gaze,

every half-love
for sustenance.

I have swallowed attention like a meal,
let it sit heavy in my stomach,
convinced myself it would keep me warm
through the night.

But love given in halves
is not love,
and I have been so desperate to be fed
that I have settled for things
that were never meant to nourish me.

I have loved people
in the way starving things love—
desperate, frantic,
willing to tear myself apart
just for a taste.
I have chewed my own fingers down to the bone
just to have something to hold onto.
I have stretched myself wide,
made a feast of my own body,
laid myself out like an offering.

Take this.
Take me.
Just don't leave me empty.

I have mistaken emptiness for romance.
I have mistaken longing for proof.

If I want you this badly,
if I ache this much in your absence,
if I feel hollow when you are gone—

then surely, surely, this must mean something.

Surely the ache is evidence.

But hunger does not mean the meal is real.
Wanting does not mean being wanted.

I have loved like something desperate,
something wild-eyed,
something abandoned too long in a locked room.

I have clung to the first hands that reached for me,
convinced myself they were safe
just because they were there.
I have ignored the way they loosened their grip,
ignored the way they recoiled
when I pulled too close.

I tell myself I am just affectionate.
That I am soft.
That I am full of love.

But the truth is—
I am just afraid of starving again.

And so I do not ask for too much.
I do not take more than what is offered.
I do not demand or expect
or reach beyond the limits
of what they are willing to give.

I take the crumbs
and convince myself they are enough.
I take silence
and convince myself it is space—

that it is patience,
that it is a sign of something steady.

I tell myself
this is what love is supposed to feel like—
a slow burn,
a lingering ache,
a hollow that never quite fills.

I do not question
why I am always the one who stays hungry.
I do not question
why love has never felt like something solid in my hands.

But I am starting to.

I am starting to wonder
if love should not feel like this.
If it should not feel like scarcity,
like rationing,
like keeping track
of who last reached first.

I am starting to wonder
if love should not feel like waiting by an empty plate,
hoping someone remembers to feed me.

I am starting to wonder
what it would be like
to leave the table altogether.

What it would be like
to let myself starve a little longer—
just long enough to remember
that I was never meant

to survive off scraps.

What it would be like
to build a hunger for something real.

Something whole.
Something that does not leave me empty.

The First Education

The first time I saw sex
wasn't tenderness.
It was choreography—
fast, breathless,
like everyone was late
for something sacred.

I learned early
that intimacy meant performance.
That wanting was a sprint,
not a slow reach across the dark.
That pleasure was proof,
and women were proof of it.

I was too young
to understand what I was learning,
but my body took notes anyway.

It learned the rhythm
of pretending.
It learned that connection
came with angles,
that desire was supposed to look like hunger,
and hunger was supposed to hurt.

We grew up on screens
that showed everything
except what mattered—

no build, no laughter,
no holy pause
between touch and touch.

Just bodies colliding,
as if closeness could be manufactured
on demand.

And then we entered the world
with those scripts
burning behind our eyes—
believing love should be instant,
believing depth was optional,
believing people were consumable.

I tried to fit inside that pace.
I tried to make it mean something.

But my mind is too slow,
too sacred,
too human
for that kind of forgetting.

I can't turn myself
into a spectacle.
I can't kiss
without memory.
I can't fuck
without consequence.

I'm not built for casual.
The complexities of me refuse it—
the ache, the afterthought,
the pretending not to care.

I want the trembling,
the build-up,
the recognition
that we are two souls
and not just two scenes.

Maybe that makes me outdated.
Maybe that makes me soft.

But I don't want to be consumed.
I want to be known.

The Slow Flood

I do not remember the first time I felt ashamed.
Only that it came quietly.

A slow thing,
a creeping thing,
like water filling a room inch by inch,
and me, standing there,
watching it rise.

I only remember knowing.
Knowing that my body
was something to be controlled,
something to be measured,
something to be fixed.

It happened in mirrors—
in reflections caught in passing,
in the way fabric clung
in places I did not want it to,
in the way hands traced their own outlines,
pressing into softness
and waiting for it to disappear.

It happened in dressing rooms.
In the fluorescent hum
of overhead lights,
where the body became something
separate from the self—

something to be pinched,
adjusted,
re-evaluated,
something unworthy
of taking up space.

It happened in whispers.
In the way women spoke of their own bodies
like open wounds.

In the way they smiled
when they ate nothing at all.

In the way hunger became a virtue—
became something to be admired.

I learned that smaller was safer.
That shrinking meant approval.
That desire and disgust
could live in the same breath.

And so I held myself tightly.
I learned not to trust hunger.
I learned to step lightly,
to apologize
for the space I took up,
to disappear just enough
to be loved.

Anatomy of a Lie

I learned young
that flesh could betray you.
That softness could be a sin.

That a body is not a home,
but a thing to be pruned,
measured,
held up to the light
and found lacking.

I grew,
and the question grew with me.
It tangled itself
in the sinew of my ribs,
became a thing with weight,
became a thing I carried.

Was I always meant
to hold myself so tightly?
To shrink until I fit
in someone's palm?
To fold myself
into something more manageable,
more likable,
more lovable?

I touch my body now—
older hands, familiar bones—

and wonder
if I was ever meant
to stay whole.

I want the kind of closeness
where someone knows
how I like my orange peeled.

Where they don't ask,
they just do it,
and hand me the piece
I always save for last.

What Color Is Silence?

When I was small,
I believed that maybe—
just maybe—
a pair of shiny scissors
could snip the edges
of this tight, suffocating casing,
free me from the twisted knot
of my own breath,
loosen the press of my bones
against the thick hush of my skin.

The question thrummed
in my ribcage:
If I cut here—
if I slice this trembling fold,
this paper-thin border—
would everything I hide inside
pour out like confessions
rushing from torn seams?

I imagined the way
the flesh might part,
like splitting a peach,
its soft fuzz surrendering
to the blade's cold insistence.

A macabre curiosity—
a child's daydream of unraveling—

to see what color my silence was
once it spilled free.

Would it be bright
as a neon cry?
A sudden gush
of burning scarlet
on the bathroom tile,
sticky truths
I never spoke aloud?

Or would it be dark and slow,
seeping secrets
that needed the air
to become real?

In that hush
between steel and skin,
I saw possibility—
a raw unveiling of the being
caged beneath my ribs,
the gnawing fear
that lived in my lungs,
the coil of shame
tucked behind my heart.

All pinned down,
like insects under glass.

Childhood question
turned obsession,
throbbing at the back of my skull:

Could I peel back each layer,
unfold the ghost I'd become,

until everything about me
was wide open,
unhidden,
streaming out in thick rivulets
for all to see—

Only then, I thought,
would they see the real me.
The one trapped beneath.
The one I believed
might finally be beautiful,
once I carved her free.

The Year I Didn't Make a Wish

The candles were still burning
when I decided to be good
instead of happy.

Before the singing was over,
before the wax dripped down the sides,
I'd already promised myself
I wouldn't eat the cake.

Not because I didn't want it—
God, I wanted it—
but because I'd already started
counting calories instead of candles,
measuring worth in what I could resist
instead of what I could enjoy.

That year, my t-shirts
started pulling tighter.
The bows on my dresses
refused to knot neatly.

My mother's hands
lingered longer at my shoulders
when she zipped me up,
her mouth pressed thin,
as if my growing
was something that could be corrected
if she caught it in time.

I learned the shape of my body
before I learned long division.
I learned how to cross my arms
without thinking,
how to angle my body in photos,
how to sit so my stomach
didn't fold
in the wrong places.

Some girls got to stay girls longer.
Got to smear frosting
across their lips,
lean back and laugh
with their mouths still full.

Got to blow out candles
without wishing
for a different body,
without bargaining in silence
for thinner arms
or a smaller waist.

I don't remember
what I asked for that year.

I only remember
the way the frosting looked—
bright and soft,
piped into perfect scallops,
like something meant
to be ruined with joy.

And how I sat there,
telling myself

I didn't want it.

That year,
I didn't make a wish.
I just blew out the candles
and watched the smoke curl away,
taking something with it
I would spend years
trying to get back.

Before I Was a Body, I Was a Girl

Before I was a body,
I was a girl.

And no one warned me
they would try to make those two things different—
that I would mourn one
in order to survive in the other.

That girl didn't flinch when she ran.
Didn't tug her shirt down before standing up.
She laughed with her whole face—
teeth showing, belly rising.
She didn't ask if it was too much.

But then came the mirrors.
The measuring.
The boys who looked past her
unless she was shrinking.
The compliments that felt like conditions:
"you'd be so pretty if..."
"if you just lost a little..."
"if you wore it like this..."

So I became the body.

Tried to tuck the girl beneath the flesh—
quiet her, starve her, smooth her edges
until she looked easier to love.

But she never left.
She just got quieter.
Waited behind my ribs,
watching me trade softness for silence,
watching me mistake obedience for growth.

And still—
sometimes in the shower,
sometimes mid-laugh—
I feel her pushing through.
Not asking to be seen.
Just refusing to stay buried.

Before I was a body,
I was a girl.

And I think I miss her.
I think I owe her
more than what I became
to survive.

I still press my fingers
into the soft of my stomach,
as if I'm checking for proof
that I exist.

I Do Not Know How to Eat Without Shame

I do not remember a time
before hunger was a performance.

Before eating became an act of failure,
before fullness felt like something
to apologize for.

I learned early
how to make meals disappear—
not just in hunger,
but in secrecy,
in shame.

A handful of crackers
crumbled between my fingers,
swallowed dry and fast,
because to eat slowly
is to acknowledge desire.
Because to chew too long
is to taste,
and to taste is to want,
and to want
is to lose control.

I have eaten standing over the sink.
I have eaten in cars, in bathrooms, in closets,
in the dark, in the silence, in the guilt.

I have let hunger sit inside me
like a secret,
have let it hollow me out
like a cavern,
have mistaken it for virtue,
have mistaken it for beauty.

I have licked salt from my palm
to trick my body into thinking
it was fed.

I have pressed my stomach
flat against the mattress,
wondering if I could will it away.

I have let my body eat itself—
gnawed at my own reserves
until my skin bruised easy,
until my nails turned brittle,
until I felt a quiet, eerie lightness,
like maybe if I kept going,
I would just
float away.

I have binged until my ribs ached,
until my skin felt too tight,
until my stomach begged for mercy.

I have wept on the bathroom floor,
knelt before porcelain like an altar,
wondered if my fingers
could undo my mistakes.

I have spent years
negotiating my existence—

promising myself I'd be worth something
if I could just be less.

Less stomach.
Less thighs.
Less flesh to be touched.
Less hunger to be named.

I have stepped on scales
and let them decide my mood,
let numbers tell me
whether or not I deserved joy.

I have stood in front of mirrors
and hated the way my skin
insisted on clinging to my bones.

But I know better now.
I know my body is mine—
not a promise to keep,
not a debt to pay,
not an apology waiting to be made.

I know fullness is not failure.
I know hunger is not virtue.

And still—
some days,
I have to remind myself.

Armor

A handful of something—
something that can be justified,
something that can be forgotten.

A bite.
A taste.
A test.

Then another.
And another.

Then it is no longer about hunger.
It is about urgency.
It is about desperation.
It is about filling the gaps
before they swallow me whole.

I eat like I am building armor.
Like I am stacking bricks,
layering myself against the world.
I eat so the soft parts of me are protected.
I eat so there is something
between me and them.
I eat so there is a reason
for the shame I already feel.

I do not stop when I am full.
I do not stop

when my stomach begs for mercy.
I do not stop
when my skin pulls tight,
when my breath is shallow,
when the guilt starts to slither in.

I do not stop
until I am safe.
Until I am numb.

Because numb is better than empty.
Because full is better than craving.
Because if I eat enough,
maybe the wanting will go away.

I eat to disappear.
And then I eat
to exist again.

I eat like I am trying
to make myself undeniable—
like if there is more of me,
maybe I will finally take up enough space
to be noticed.
To be real.
To be worthy.

And after—
after the last bite,
after the last scrape of teeth against metal,
after the body swells with regret—

I sit in it.

I press my hands to my stomach,

feel the weight, the proof, the consequence.
I tell myself this is the last time.
That next time I will be better.
That next time I will be stronger.

But next time always comes.
And next time
always swallows me whole.

Food Noise

There is a sound that lives in my mouth late at night—
a small, animal clamor that eats the room.

It is not hunger.
It is a thing that arrives with anger, boredom, loneliness,
the TV glow.
A radio tuned to the worst station.

I tell myself I will stop.
I say the things I'm supposed to say:
drink water, breathe, count to ten.
I set bowls like boundaries.

But bowls are polite;
the noise is not.

It bangs on the inside of my skull
until my hands move first,
before my brain.

I eat as if I am trying
to prove the world wrong—
as if swallowing could fill the places
that keep whispering
I'm too much,
not enough,
wrong.

84

I shovel sugar like repentance.
I eat white things
to make myself small.

The kitchen light
is a confession booth.
The wrapper clicks
like an accusation.

After, the shame arrives—
heavy and fluorescent,
a tide that rewrites
my every thought.

I hate myself
with a clarity
that smells like bleach.

I vow to be better,
to be thinner,
to be quieter—
and the next night
the same broadcast returns,
louder.

It is a cycle
with its own gravity.

Sometimes I imagine
ripping the noise out by the root:
dramatic gestures,
new rules,
a clean slate.

But recovery is never dramatic.

It is stubborn,
low-grade work—
a life rewritten
in teaspoons
and failed promises.

I have learned small mercies:
grocery lists in hand,
a friend to answer at midnight,
a text I write
and never send.

I have learned
to ask my hands to wait.
To name the feeling
before it becomes food.

There are days
I let myself be present
with the want:
I put my palm to my throat
and say out loud,
This is craving.
This is not a sentence.

I try to hold tenderness
for the girl who eats
to numb the ache
she could not name.

She did not choose shame;
she chose survival.
She chose the only thing
that worked then.

But the noise is loud
and apologetic
and relentless.

It says:
you failed.
you will fail again.
you are unfixable.

And yet—
there is a crack in that voice now,
a place where compassion
can slip through.

There is a hand
that does not point
but stays.

There are things I can do
that feel like stitches:
small,
ugly,
honest.

So I am learning
to sit with the ache
without stuffing it whole.
To name the hunger
that is not food.
To breathe into the hollow.
To let the kitchen
be a room
and not a verdict.

I still make mistakes.

I still wake
to the outline of the wrapper
like a map
at my bedside.

But sometimes—
sometimes—
the noise quiets enough
for a single, quiet breath
to fit between the pieces of me.

And that breath
is not victory.
It's a start.

Built for Rotting

Fear—
it rots in my stomach,
turns my insides septic.

It chews at the lining of my gut,
makes a meal of my nerves,
stretches itself long and lazy beneath my ribs,
licking its teeth.

And regret—
I think regret lives in the marrow.
A sickness in my bones.
A low-grade fever that never quite breaks.

I regret the way I have feared.
How I have lived small,
kept my hands clean,
tucked my desires into the lining of my pockets
like lint,
let them gather and tangle.

I regret the things I have not done
more than the things I have.
I regret not splitting myself open on experience,
not pressing my fingers to the flame,
not letting something ruin me
just to see if I could crawl out of the wreckage.

Would I have crawled out?
Or would I have let the fire have me?
I think about that.
I think about that a lot.

I fear that I was never built for ruin—
that I was only built for rotting.
With time, fear gets heavier.
It calcifies,
becomes something solid,
something with a pulse.

I am too aware of myself,
of the way I move through space,
the weight of my presence in a room,
the static that follows in my wake.

And so I shrink.
I dull the edges.
I pull myself inward
like something skinned alive.

I do not rock the boat—
God, no—
I sit so still
I don't even breathe too hard.

And still, the current pulls me out.
Further
Further.

Until the shore is a mirage,
a forgotten thing,
a fever dream I barely remember.
My body sways

in the nothingness of it all.

I fear I have lost my paddle.
Or maybe I was never given one.

Maybe I have been stranded from the start—
flailing,
pretending I knew what I was doing
when I have been gulping down saltwater,
letting the sea rot my teeth out.

My gums, soft.
My mouth, raw.
Maybe I was never meant to reach land at all.
Maybe I am not even supposed to try.

And I fear—
God, I fear that fear is all I have left.
That I have let it eat too much of me.
That I have become it.

I wake up with it stretched across my chest,
pressing me into the sheets
like a second skin.

I breathe it in with the morning air,
let it sit heavy in my stomach,
let it fill my lungs
until I am drunk on it,
sick with it.

And then regret comes,
lurching up like something rotten,
sitting sour on my tongue.
I regret how far behind I am.

I regret the years I have wasted
waiting for someone to tell me
I am allowed to want, to take,
to run headfirst
into something beautiful
and jagged
and alive.

I regret that I needed to be told at all.
I regret how long I have sat in this.

And I have sat.
I have swelled in it.
I have gorged myself on fear,
swallowed it whole,
let it line my throat,
let it fill the hollows of my body
like insulation.

I have hoarded it,
stored it away beneath my skin,
carved out room for more.

I let it fester,
let it seep into my pores,
let it hollow me out.

I regret what I have done to my body.
Or maybe I regret
what I have let it become.

Because the fear is not just inside me anymore.
It has made a home in my flesh—
pulled my skin too tight,
stretched it thin like wet paper,

left fingerprints
on the insides of my wrists,
pressed its teeth
into the meat of my thighs,
made a ruin
of my reflection.

I touch my body
and I do not recognize it.
I look at my hands
and they do not feel like mine.
I do not know what I have done to them.
Or maybe I do,
and I just do not want to say it.

It does not just sink in.
It burrows.
It burrows deep.

Beyond the skin.
Beyond the muscle.

It is in my blood.
It is in my teeth.
It is in my breath.
I am afraid to breathe too hard,
in case the fear spills out.
I am afraid it has fused with my bones.
I am afraid
I am already gone.

And still, I wait.

For what?

For someone to tell me I can still swim?
For the tide to return me to shore?
For the fear to dissolve in the sun?

Or maybe—
maybe I am waiting
for the ocean to finally
take me under.

Almost Beautiful

There is a moment,
right after the last sob leaves your body,
where everything is quiet.

The body still hiccupping,
breath raw, throat thick.
Your ribs stretched too thin,
your chest hollow
but somehow heavier.

You catch your reflection—
face wet, swollen,
ugly in a way
that almost makes you feel beautiful.

There is an awful kind of beauty in it.
A sick, holy kind of relief.
Like the body has finally been wrung out, emptied—
like you've finally poured out all the ache
pressing against your ribs.

The pain is still there, yes—
but now it is manageable,
understandable,
yours.

No longer blooming behind your eyes.
No longer pressing at the back of your throat

like a swallowed scream.
No longer clogging
the delicate machinery of you.

And the strangest part?

You almost want to cry again.
Just to stay in this moment.
Just to keep yourself inside the wreckage,
because here, everything is sharp enough to touch.

The ache has weight.
The silence has texture.
Your body, your ruin, your face—
all of it unbearably real.

You wipe your face
with the back of your hand—
skin slick, damp, feverish.

Your lips are bitten red.
Your nose burns.
Your eyelashes stick together
like tiny, exhausted fists.

You don't need a mirror
to know what you look like.

Ruin.

There is something strangely satisfying about it, isn't there?
The aftermath of an exorcism.
The way pain leaves its trace
not just inside you
but on you, as if to say:

Here. This was real.
Here. This is what you survived.

But your body doesn't let go easily.
Even when the sobs are gone,
your ribs still ache.
Your stomach still clenches.
Your fingertips pulse
like tiny aftershocks.

The storm may have passed,
but your body remembers the thunder.

And still—
you linger in the pause.

You don't wash your face right away.
You let the tears dry in streaks.
You sit with the damp heat of your own skin.
You linger in the wreckage
before cleaning it up.

Because this—
this is the closest you've come to honesty all week.
This is the kind of clarity
that only arrives
when you've been cracked open.

Maybe that's why you let yourself break like this.
Why you don't stop it.
Why you let the crying take you under,
why you let yourself be ruined by it.

Because in the moment after—

when your body is soft and spent,
when the world is too quiet,
when the grief has finally bled itself out—
you feel pure.

You feel emptied.
You feel like something newly born.

And you know it won't last.
Tomorrow—
maybe even in an hour—
you will be full of ache again.

The lump will return to your throat
like an old, familiar guest.
You will carry it.
You will let it sit.
You will let it rot inside you
until it needs to come out again.

And then you will cry.
And then you will return here—

to this pause,
to this ruin,
to this sharp, unbearable, holy quiet.

And you will sit with it,
pressing your fingers to your swollen lips,
staring at your own exhausted reflection,
thinking what you'll never say out loud:

God, I almost feel beautiful.

Desire's Muddy Feet

desire doesn't wait for permission.
it shows up dripping, barefoot,
tracking mud through every room of me.

sometimes I let it.
sometimes I clean until morning.

Foreign Body

It's small.
Almost invisible.

A needle-thin fragment
buried just beneath the skin.

If I press down,
I can feel it shift—
a sharp thing
beneath soft flesh.

It does not belong to me.
And yet,
it is inside me.

I should pull it out.
I know this.

But there's something
about the way it sits there—
the way my body
has wrapped itself around it,
hesitant, unsure
whether to reject
or absorb.

My skin puckers,
tightens,

swells.

It reddens around the edges.
It throbs when I touch it.

A warning.
A wound
that has not yet become one.

I know it will hurt me.
And I will let it.

For a while.

Until I'm clawing at the skin,
searching for the source of pain—
only to find
it's already become
a part of me.

Flesh

There are parts of me
I only see in mirrors angled wrong.

The folds that gather
when I sit too long.
The shadows that bloom beneath my arms,
blue-black whispers in the creases.

The skin that ripples like water
across my thighs,
cellulite catching the light
like it has something to confess.

I imagine your eyes finding them
before your hands do.
Imagine your mouth going quiet—
not out of cruelty,
but out of not knowing what to say.

And I hear it then—
the chorus I've carried since childhood:
too much,
too soft,
too heavy,
not worth holding.

Every stretch mark
is handwriting across my belly,

scribbled proof of how far I've stretched,
how much space I've dared to take.

Every roll feels like a verdict.
Every bruise-colored patch of skin
like shame stitched permanent
into my body.

I stand under fluorescent lights
and wonder what you'd see
if you looked too close.

Would you notice the dip in my back
where fat gathers like a secret?
Would you measure my arms
against girls who inherited thinness
like a birthright?
Would you trace the rise of my belly
and mistake softness for failure?

The cruelest part
isn't what you might see.
It's what I've already told myself.

The phantom judgments.
The imagined recoils.
The silence I've rehearsed
a thousand times.

The fear that my body, once revealed,
will be the punchline
I can't escape.

But flesh is not an apology.

These marks are not accidents—
they are cartography.
Every line a survival.
Every bruise a history.
Every fold a testament:

I lived.
I grew.
I stayed.

So if you look,
look honestly.

See the body as it is—
not a flaw to correct,
not a riddle to solve,
but a living archive
of everything I've endured.

This is my flesh.
It trembles.
It scars.
It resists

It holds me.

And whether or not you can bear it—
it will go on
holding me still

The Body I Tried to Punish

I have starved her.
I have stuffed her.
I have pinched and pulled
and cursed her name.

I have called her lazy
when she begged for rest,
ugly when she softened,
disgusting
when she simply existed.

I have waged war
against the only thing
that ever tried
to keep me alive.

Still, she stayed.

She healed
when I wouldn't.
She forgave me
before I ever asked.

Every bruise faded.
Every scar closed.
Every morning,
she began again
as if I hadn't tried

to break her
the night before.

And now,
when I touch the curve
of my stomach,
when I see the stretch
of my thighs in sunlight,
I whisper an apology
that feels too small.

I tell her
I didn't know better.
I tell her
I'm learning.

I tell her thank you
for never giving up on me
even when I did.

III — THE BODY

friendship · self-witness · survival

Mirror or Mouth

Sometimes I couldn't tell
if I wanted her lipstick
or the mouth wearing it.
If I wanted her waist
or my hands around it.

If I wanted her hair
or the chance to pull it loose,
watching her become messy in my hands.

I told myself it was admiration.
That it was only envy.
That the ache in my stomach
was just another reminder
of everything I wasn't.

But why did my chest tighten
when she leaned too close?
Why did I memorize
the freckles on her collarbone
like they were mine to claim?
Why did I dream of her laugh
in the dark
and wake up flushed,
like I'd been caught?

Maybe girlhood gave me
the wrong vocabulary.

It taught me how to compete,
how to shrink beside beauty,
but not how to name the heat
that rose in my body
when beauty touched my hand.

So I swallowed it.
Called it jealousy.
Called it nothing.

But my body knew better.
It hummed in the spaces between us.
It reached before I did.
It wanted
what I was too afraid
to let myself want.

And maybe that's why
I still look at women
and wonder if the hunger in me
is longing
or reflection.

If I wanted to *be* her—
or if, all along,
I just wanted
beneath her.

Body at Peace

I don't wake up hating it anymore.
The body.
The noise.
The way it takes up space before I can think.

Some mornings I still catch myself
pinching the softness,
reaching for the old ritual of apology.
But then I stop.
I press my palm to my stomach—
warm, alive, here—
and whisper, *stay.*

Peace isn't the absence of ache.
It's the decision to stop punishing yourself
for being a person.

I make coffee slowly.
I stretch without counting calories.
I buy clothes that fit the body I have,
not the one I'm waiting for.

The mirror and I don't fight anymore;
we just look at each other—
two old friends finally out of excuses.

Some days, peace is barely a whisper.
Some days, it fills the whole room.

But it's mine now—
this fragile, borrowed thing.
And for the first time,
I believe I might keep it.

When Friends Were Mirrors

No one tells you
how friendship can undo you.

How sitting next to someone you love
can make you hate yourself harder.

I remember the way they entered a room—
effortless,
like the world had been saving them a seat.

The way laughter stuck to them
and followed them out the door.

And I thought:
if I were thinner, louder, softer, brighter—
anything but this—
maybe I could earn
what seemed to come naturally to them.

It wasn't their fault.
They never asked me to disappear.
They never pointed at the parts of me
I tore apart in the mirror each night.

But proximity has a way of distorting things.
Beside them,
I became a shadow of myself—
all warped angles and echoes,

waiting for someone to notice
what I already feared.

I carried that mirror everywhere.
Into conversations,
into photographs,
into the silence that grew between us.

It was easier to believe I was less,
easier to let comparison do the talking,
than admit I was bleeding out
in a friendship that never meant me harm.

Still, I loved them.
Loved them in the kind of way
that tasted like envy and devotion at once.

And maybe that's the thing no one says out loud—
that jealousy can live in the same room as love,
that admiration can scrape you raw
if you don't know how to hold yourself yet.

I don't hold it against them.
Not anymore.
They were never the villain.
The war was always with myself.

And now, years later,
I can see what I couldn't then:
that friendships are mirrors,
and some will reflect the best in you,
while others force you to face
the parts you'd rather bury.

Both are teachers.

Both are love, in their own flawed way.

And maybe the most grown thing I can say is this:
I wish them well.

Even the ones who made me doubt myself.
Even the ones who left me lonelier
in my own skin.

Because looking back,
they gave me something too—
the chance to see where I ended
and where they began.

The chance to learn
that envy is a shadow,
but shadows can only exist in light.

I know myself better now.
I know that love is not a competition,
that worth is not a limited resource.

I know that the mirror they held up
was never the truth of me—
only the lesson I needed
to finally face my own reflection
without flinching.

So when I think of them now,
I don't feel small.

I feel grateful.

For the mirror,
for the ache,

for the proof that even the hardest friendships
can leave you more whole
than they found you.

For the Friends Who Stayed

Not all love wears rings.

Some love looks like a couch cushion
that remembers the weight of your body.

Some love looks like a car idling in the driveway
long after midnight,
waiting until you're ready to go inside.

This is the love that doesn't ask you to earn it.
The love that shows up with soup when you're sick
and stays long enough to make sure you eat it.

The love that knows your mother's maiden name,
your old passwords,
the color of the dress you swore you'd never wear again.

Some people chase grand gestures.
But this love lives in smaller rooms—
in borrowed sweatshirts,
split Uber fares,
the familiar corner of the bar where you always end up,
in the phone call where nothing is wrong,
and still they stay on the line.

You thought you were missing out
because you didn't have the romance—
the hand to hold under restaurant tables,

the kisses goodnight at someone else's door.

But you had this.

The devotion that doesn't brag about itself,
doesn't take photos,
doesn't need proof.
And maybe—
that's what saved you.

Because when the heartbreaks came,
when the family left,
when the nights turned cruel and endless,
this love was already in the room.

Sitting cross-legged on the floor.
Pouring another drink.
Listening to the same story for the hundredth time
like it was brand new.

So no, not all love wears rings.

Some love has keys to your apartment.
Some love has memorized the way you cry.
Some love has kept you alive—
quietly, faithfully—
and asked for nothing back
but the chance
to stay.

Sometimes I think my laugh is too loud.
Then I remember — so is thunder.
And no one asks thunder to be quieter.

Body in Motion

You learn the dialect of your body slowly—
in the way your lungs answer the stair,
in the low protest of your knees after a run,
in the sudden bloom beneath your ribs
when a song you love finds you.

Your soles press into the ground and notice:
muscle remembering gravity,
weight not as shame but as anchor—
an old, loyal reminder that you are still here.

You lift your arms and the air yields;
it parts like water, like recognition.
You begin with tiny gestures—
a shoulder loosening,
a toe curling against the floor,
a hip whispering yes.

You let your chest soften without permission.
You practice laughing with your whole mouth,
reckless and bright,
just to hear what your body sounds like
when it rejoices.

There is tenderness in it—
your palm resting at your sternum,
feeling the steady insistence
of a life that keeps choosing you.

So move.
Not for the mirror.
Not for the like.
Not for the story someone else will tell about you.

Move because your body is a voice
and you have kept it silent too long.
Move because returning to yourself
is work worth doing in the daylight.

Move because love is a practice
you can do with your whole skin on.

You will learn the grammar of your body in time—
how it apologizes,
how it consents,
how it remembers.

Until then—
press your hand down.
Breathe.
Begin again.

Speak From The Belly

From the belly, I speak.
From the place that clenches first—
that warns not safe,
that remembers every silence
I ever swallowed.

This belly has held hunger.
This belly has held shame.
This belly has held secrets
I feared would rot me from the inside.
And still—
it is where the voice begins.

Not in the throat,
where words get dressed up polite.
Not in the head,
where fear edits every syllable.
The voice begins deeper—
where breath becomes heat,
where trembling still counts as alive.

From the belly, I speak.
Even when it quivers.
Even when the room prefers me quiet.
Even when my own body whispers *hide*.

I speak because silence was never safety.
It was a coffin

I climbed into willingly.

So let it shake.
Let it burn.
Let the sound rise raw and unpretty.
Let it split the air—
thunder with no permission.

From the belly, I speak.
From the wound.
From the pulse.
From the hunger that never learned to disappear.

And if you hear me—
let it wake something in you.
Let your belly answer mine.
Let your voice come trembling
through your teeth.

From the belly,
we speak.

Forgive Me If I Say Something Stupid

Forgive me if I say something stupid.
I'm not good at being here—
not fully, not yet.

I overthink eye contact,
apologize too quickly,
rehearse lines that never land quite right.
I want to be present — I do —
but my mind keeps dragging me back to the mirror,
to the moment I said too much,
or not enough.

So if I fumble,
if I laugh too loud
or go quiet all at once,
forgive me if I'm not graceful yet.
If I take up space in uneven ways.

I've spent so long editing myself
that I don't always know what it sounds like
to speak without fearing the echo.
I'm still learning how to be a person in real time—
still untangling my words from the static in my head.

If I talk too fast,
if I freeze mid-sentence like a glitch,
know it's not indifference.
It's fear—

the kind that lives in the body,
that burns behind the knees,
that tightens in the jaw.

But I'm here.
Even if I don't know how to show it.
Even if I say something stupid.
Even if I don't get it right
the first time.

I laugh in places I should cry.
It feels less like joy,
more like camouflage.

Lies I Tell Myself in My Own Diary

I write it down,
so it must be true.
That's the rule.
That's the whole point of a diary, isn't it?
To confess.
To be honest.
And yet—I lie.

I lie boldly, deliberately, beautifully.
I lie so well I almost believe myself.

I write: I'm doing better.
And then I cancel plans,
leave messages unanswered,
watch another day slip through my fingers
like it was never mine to hold.
I write: I don't mind being alone.
And then I fall asleep to the TV
so I don't have to hear the quiet.
I stand in the kitchen long enough
to pretend I'm waiting for someone—
not avoiding my own reflection.

I write: *I am not tired.*
And then I wake up exhausted,
carrying the same unfinished thoughts
into another morning.

I write: *I am trying.*
And then the dishes stack,
emails sour in my inbox,
dinner becomes crackers over the sink.

I write: *I don't care anymore.*
And then I replay conversations from five years ago
like they still owe me closure.

I write: *I'm over it.*
And then I go back—
back to old habits,
back to people who never chose me,
back to waiting for something
that never arrives.

I write: *I am healing.*
And then I pick at the scab
just to see if it still bleeds.

I lie to myself in my own diary.
Not out of cruelty—
but out of hope.

Because maybe I'm not writing what's true.
Maybe I'm writing what I need to believe.
Maybe every line is a wish in disguise,
a version of me I'm still becoming.

And maybe that's enough.
Maybe the lie is a bridge.
Maybe the lie is a beginning.
Maybe if I keep writing it,
one day I won't be lying at all.

Falling for Myself

The way I caught my reflection one morning
and didn't look away first.
The way my laugh slipped out,
louder than I meant,
and I let it stay.

Falling for myself wasn't sudden.
It was the mornings I brewed coffee the way I like it,
even if no one else would drink it that way.
It was buying flowers for my own table,
just because they made me smile.
It was walking into a room
without checking who might be watching.

For so long I measured myself against outlines—
who I thought I should be,
who I thought would be easier to love.
But somewhere along the way,
I started wanting the version of me
that actually exists.

The one with messy hair and stubborn opinions.
The one who overthinks but still shows up.
The one who doesn't get everything right,
but gets back up anyway.

Falling for myself feels like exhaling—
like finally choosing the person

who's been here all along.

And maybe this is what love really is:
not changing to be chosen,
but choosing to stay
right here,
with myself.

House Rules

Rule: Don't want too loudly.
New rule: Want so big the walls remember your echo.

Rule: Shrink your laugh.
New rule: Let it spill, unbuttoned, across the whole room.

Rule: Be grateful for crumbs.
New rule: Leave the table. Build your own feast.

Rule: Keep secrets that bruise you.
New rule: Drag them into daylight. Name them until they lose their teeth.

Rule: Be polite when they cut you down.
New rule: Grow taller. Make them crane their necks to reach you.

Rule: Be small, be quiet, be sweet.
New rule: Take up the street.
Take up the sky.
Take up **everything** they said you couldn't.

130

The problem is I want to be both unforgettable
and completely unknown.
Maybe that's what it means
to be real —
to live in the tension
between exposure and mystery.

The Version That's Easiest to Hold

Sometimes I wonder if anyone actually sees me.
Truly sees me—not the version I parade around in soft light and passable charm.
Not the clever girl. Not the sad girl.
Not the one who's always hovering somewhere between a joke
and a confession.

The real me.
The one who flinches when she's asked anything too close to the truth.

I sit across from people who say they love me,
but they never ask the right questions.
Never dig past the polish.
Never notice the twitch in my smile
when I lie and say I'm fine.

Sometimes I feel like I'm standing behind glass—
pressed up against it,
breath fogging the surface—
watching the world touch reflections of me
instead of the real thing.

No one's curious.
No one asks what I was like as a child,
or what songs make me cry,
or why I always leave parties without saying goodbye.
They just accept the version that's easiest to hold.

No one asks.
Not really.
Not the things that matter.
Not what keeps me up,
or what I daydream about when it rains,
or why I laugh before I cry.

I want someone to press their hands
to the parts of me I hide.
To knock on the locked doors.
To ask anyway.
To stay anyway.

There Is No Right Time

There is no perfect morning where you wake up
and feel brave enough,
or certain enough,
or ready enough
to begin.

No grand unveiling
where you finally become the version of yourself
you always swore you'd wait for.

You will wait forever
if you are waiting to feel ready.
You will wait until your body looks different in the mirror.
Until your voice sounds better in the air.
Until fear shrinks small enough to step over.
Until someone gives you permission to exist.

But the truth is—
no one is coming.
No one is going to tap you on the shoulder and say,
Now. Now is the moment you start living.

Because it has always been now.
And you will waste lifetimes waiting—
to wear the dress,
to take the picture,
to love yourself
the way you were supposed to all along.

You will watch days slip through your fingers like sand,
lost to hesitation,
to doubt,
to the lie that you are not yet enough.
There is no finish line where you are finally worthy.
No ceremony where the universe says,
Congratulations. You have arrived.

You have to choose it.
You have to reach with trembling hands.
You have to let it be messy
and take it anyway.
Because time does not care if you are waiting.
Because the moment will pass.

And one day,
you will look back and ache
for all the times
you didn't let yourself have what was already yours.

So do it now.
Not because you are fearless.
Not because you are ready.
But because the wanting itself
is proof you are alive.

Hesitation will hollow you.
Trying—even trembling—will build you.

Start before you think you deserve to.
Begin before the mirror agrees with you.
Claim it while your hands are still shaking.

Because one day you will thank yourself

for starting anyway.

And that—
more than readiness—
is what carries you forward.

IV — THE LINEAGE

family · inheritance · time

I Have My Mother's Nose

I have my mother's nose.
The same curve, the same steady bridge—
a feature passed down like a secret.

When I look at it now,
I don't see something to fix.
I see her.
Her laughter folded into the slope.
Her resilience anchored in the line.
The girl she was before me,
the woman she became after—
all of it carried here,
right in the center of my face.

And it doesn't end with her.
I catch my grandmother's defiance in my brow,
my father's tenderness in the tilt of my smile.
My reflection is not just mine—
it's an archive.
Proof of the people who lived, who loved,
who survived long enough
to leave themselves behind in me.

So when I meet my own eyes in the mirror,
I try to love what I see.
Because it isn't just me staring back.
It's my mother.
It's my grandmother.

It's every story, every wound, every quiet victory
that brought me here.

This face is not a flaw.
It is a lineage.
It is a legacy.
It is love,
looking back at me.

Increments

I used to help tug their feet through pajamas,
soft cotton swallowing ankles whole,
laughing when the fabric twisted,
when they kicked too hard,
when bedtime was still something they fought.

Now the hems hover above bone.
Their voices crack mid-sentence.
They don't ask for stories anymore.
They don't climb into laps without thinking.

It happens in increments—
the way childhood always does.
A sock that no longer fits.
A stuffed animal left on the couch.
A hug that feels more like a handshake
because suddenly, they're taller than me.

No one warns you about the grief
that comes with watching someone grow—
not out of your life,
but out of the smaller versions you once knew.

You don't lose them all at once.
You lose them in pieces:
an outgrown pajama,
a room that no longer needs a nightlight,
a laugh that sounds older than it should.

And still, I am grateful.
Grateful to witness the leaving.
Grateful to hold the memory of who they were
while loving who they're becoming.

Because this is what time does—
it folds, it stretches,
it asks you to loosen your grip
and keep holding on anyway.

And maybe that's the gift of it:
to mourn what's gone
while still cheering for what's ahead.
To let the child you once knew become someone new—
and love them just as fiercely
for growing beyond your arms.

Grief is love's shadow.
It follows me everywhere,
even in sunlight.

Not every leaving is betrayal.
Some departures are just proof
that time kept moving.

Growing Together, Growing Apart

It's strange, aging side by side.
One day my brother's hands were smaller than mine,
grabbing fistfuls of my sleeve—
and now they eclipse my own,
calloused and steady, the hands of a man.

My mother's face carries years
I swear weren't there before,
fine lines etching themselves like
rings inside a tree trunk—
markers of time I almost missed.

Birthdays arrive like highway exits—
too close, too fast,
no space to pull over.
We blow out candles,
watch wax slip down the sides,
laugh a little louder than we used to,
as if noise might slow the years down.

We are growing together,
yes—
but also apart.
Our lives branching like roots
born from the same soil
but stretching in different directions.

I used to think love meant closeness,

that distance meant unraveling.
But love has a longer reach than that.
It holds across states,
across changes in voice,
across faces that become
both familiar and unfamiliar at once.

And when I look at them now,
I don't see what's slipping away.
I see how time keeps us—
in their hands, their laughter, their faces—
reminding me that we are still here,
still linked by the years
we carry together.

The Things They Wanted

I think about the things they wanted
before life told them no.
Before responsibility.
Before sacrifice became second nature.
Before they learned that some dreams must be set down—
not because they weren't worthy,
but because other things needed carrying first.

I wonder if they ever look at their own hands
and think about what they could have held instead.
If they ever press their fingers to the walls of the life they built
and listen for echoes of the one they once imagined.
If they ever wake in the middle of the night,
staring at the ceiling, whispering to themselves,
was this enough?

No one warns you about this part of growing up—
that one day, you will not just grieve the childhood you lost,
you will grieve the childhood they lost too.
You will see them not just as parents, but as people.
People who once had wild, impossible dreams.
People who once ran toward something reckless and beautiful
before life told them to slow down.

You will start to understand the way time reshaped them,
the way their dreams softened at the edges,
the way they made themselves smaller, quieter, more practical—
not because they didn't want it enough,

not because they gave up,
but because they chose something else.
Because they chose to build a life
that could hold you in it.

This is not a tragedy.
This is not a story about loss.
It is a story about love.
About how some dreams are not chased, but handed down.
About how sometimes wanting more
doesn't mean reaching for something new,
but holding onto what you have.

Because love does not always look like wild ambition.
Sometimes love looks like staying.
Like showing up.
Like giving someone else a chance to dream
even bigger than you did.

And I know now—
this life they made was never small.
It was expansive in the ways that mattered.
It was full in places I didn't yet know how to see.
It was everything they had to give.

Still, some nights, I hear it—
the weight of inheritance.
Not just their blood, not just their name,
but their longing, their almosts,
the versions of themselves they never got to be.

And I wonder—
am I supposed to finish what they started?
Am I supposed to prove it wasn't all for nothing?
Am I supposed to make my life something bigger,

something more,
so they don't have to regret the things they left behind?

But the truth is this:
they did not build this life
so I could stand in the same place.
They did not work, and sacrifice,
and hold the world together
so I could hesitate at the edge of it.

I see you.
I love you.
I am because you were.

I Hoard Love in Small, Desperate Ways

I hoard love in small, desperate ways.
In the voicemails I will never delete.
In the way I trace my mother's handwriting
on old grocery lists.
In the way I press my face into sweaters
that still smell like someone I miss.

I collect love like artifacts, like proof—
as if I can stop time by keeping enough of it,
as if I can press my hands into the wet cement of a moment
and make it stay.

I hoard love in quiet things,
in things that seem unremarkable:
the last sip of coffee before someone leaves,
the weight of a hand resting on the back of my neck,
the way someone says my name like it means something,
the laugh that comes before the joke is even finished,
the fleeting, golden warmth
of a room full of people who love each other.

I store them away,
tucking them into the corners of my ribs,
lining my lungs with memory,
wrapping myself in the softness
of having once been loved.

Because one day, I know—

these moments will be all I have left.
And I want to have enough.

Time does not ask permission to pass.
It does not wait for you to be ready.

One day, you are holding your mother's hand
in a grocery store,
and then suddenly
her hands are thinner than you remember,
and you realize you don't know the last time
she ran her fingers through your hair.

One day, you are laughing with your friends
in a car at midnight,
and then suddenly
it's been years since you were all in the same room.

One day, someone is here.
And then they're not.
And all you have left is the echo of them.

So I hoard love.
I savor it.
I wring it out of every second.
I press my lips to the rim of the moment
and drink it down until there is nothing left.

I say *I love you* first.
I squeeze a little tighter when I say goodbye.
I take the picture, even if it's blurry.

Because I know one day—
I will wish I had more to hold.

Here is what I've learned:
love is fleeting, but it is not weightless.
It leaves fingerprints.
It stains.
It lingers in the fabric.
It sits heavy in the chest
long after the moment has passed.

And that is enough.
It has to be.

The Things They Remember

They don't remember the words
so much as the weight—
how it felt to hold you,
then to let you go.
Memory softens the edges,
but never the center.

Time doesn't ask permission.
It pulls us all forward—
out of pajamas, into wrinkles,
through the small doors of ourselves.
All we can do is keep walking.

Kept by Myself

Maybe I was never meant
to be chosen.
Maybe I was meant
to keep myself.
And what a gentle miracle
that has become.

V — THE BECOMING

mercy · rewriting · enoughness

Maybe I'll be single until the day I die.
But I will have loved myself,
in public and in secret,
louder and braver than anyone else ever could.

Owing It to Her

I owe it to the girl I used to be—
the one who thought disappearing
would make her easier to love.

The one who folded herself into silence,
counted crackers like currency,
smiled wide so no one would notice
how much it hurt just to stay.

I owe it to her not to vanish again.
Not to call myself unworthy
because no one said otherwise.
Not to keep waiting for permission
to want what I want.

I think about her sometimes—
small hands tugging at shirts too tight,
holding her breath in photographs,
wishing her body would shrink
before the flash went off.

She thought the world would be kinder
if she could take up less space.

But I am still here.
Still in this body.
Still carrying the ache she couldn't name,
and the hunger she was told to ignore.

I've hardened and softened both.
I've learned how to hold myself
when no one else could.

So I owe her more than apologies.
I owe her joy without conditions.
I owe her mornings where the mirror
isn't a battlefield.

I owe her laughter that doesn't sound rehearsed.
I owe her proof she was always enough—
even when she couldn't believe it.

Because if I don't keep showing up for her,
then who will?

If I don't claim her,
if I don't love her now,
then she stays the almost—
instead of becoming the always.

Some days, survival looks extraordinary.
Other days, it's brushing my teeth
and answering one message.
Both kinds count.

News That Kept Me Gentle

The news was a fire.
I watered the basil.

The news was another name.
I said mine out loud, soft as prayer.

The news was a storm.
I checked the windows, then called my mother.

The news was a war.
I mailed a birthday card anyway.

The news was a reckoning.
I shared bread with a friend.

The news kept shouting.
I kept refusing to become unkind.

We Love It Anyway

To love is to press your palm to the stove,
knowing the heat will take you eventually—
but oh, the warmth before the pain.

It's to cup water in your hands,
to adore it,
even as it slips through your fingers.

It's to hear the last note of a song
and play it again anyway.

It's to kiss with the knowledge
that one day it will be the last time.

It's knowing the flowers will wilt
and still pressing your nose to the petals.

It's knowing the sun will set
and still turning your face toward the light.

It's knowing nothing, nothing, nothing can stay—
and loving it anyway.

Love is the most reckless thing we do.
We let ourselves want.
We let ourselves need.
We let people press themselves into our ribs,
knowing one day we'll have to carve them out.

We build homes in people who cannot stay.
And still—we do it anyway.

Because what's the alternative?
To feel nothing?
To live untouched?
To never let the world carve its name into your skin?
To never know how another heartbeat
can press against your own
and make you feel more alive
than you ever thought possible?

I would rather have the ache.
I would rather have the ruin.
I would rather let love bloom,
let it decay,
let it take pieces of me with it—
if it means I get to know what it feels like
to burn for something.

Because love, in all its fleetingness,
is the only thing that's ever made me feel infinite.

Yes, love will leave.
Yes, love will break.
Yes, love will gut you and haunt you
and turn you inside out.

But for a moment—
for a beautiful, impossible, unbearable moment—
it is everything.

And I will take the wreckage.
I will take the fire.

I will take the ache that lingers in my bones—
if it means I get to feel it at all.

To love is to offer your throat to the wolf
and whisper,
I hope you don't bite down,
even as you cradle its head,
even as its breath warms your skin.

To love is to stand in the ocean,
arms outstretched,
letting the waves take and take and take—
until you're not sure if you're floating,
or drowning,
or if there's even a difference.

To love is to risk being made a ruin.
To bet your body against time
and know you will lose.

And still—
you do it anyway.

Because for the time that it's yours—
for the time you get to call it yours—
it is worth everything.

I thought healing would feel like celebration.
Mostly, it feels like practice.

Tiny Joys

I wish I could catalog every tiny joy—
peach fuzz on my wrist in sunlight,
the sound of ice cracking in a glass,
my niece's laugh when she thinks I'm ridiculous.

But the mind hoards misery like treasure.
It's unfair.

I want to remember sweetness
with the same precision.

Love has always been my sharpest hunger.
It chews at me even when I'm already full.

To Be Known

I want to be loved.
But I don't want to be looked at.
Not really—not in the ways that require honesty,
not in the ways that make me feel real.

I think I've spent most of my life making sure no one ever truly sees me.
Not because I don't want to be seen—
but because I don't know what they'll do
when they finally look close enough.
When they see the fault lines beneath the skin,
the places held too tight,
stretched too thin,
hollowed out by expectation.

To be known is to lay down my armor,
to open my palms
and trust you will not flinch
at what you find there.

What if I am
too heavy to hold,
too complicated to unravel,
too human to admire up close?

I don't know how to exist in the quiet space
between wanting and fearing,
between longing and retreat,
between the ache to be touched

and the terror of being held too tightly.

But today—right now—
with trembling hands
and uncertain breath,
I step forward.
I open myself to your eyes and ask,
softly, quietly:

can you see me beneath the layers?
can you recognize me behind the performance?
can you love me in that terrifying moment
between who I am
and who I want you to believe me to be?

I don't know if you will keep me.
I don't know if I will let you.
But in this breath,
in this fragile moment,
I am here.
I am real.
And I am hoping—aching—
that you see me,
and stay.

The Softest Thing I Did This Year

The softest thing I did this year was let myself be human.
I let the phone ring out and didn't apologize for the silence.
I ate peaches over the sink, juice running down my wrist,
and didn't wipe it away too quickly.

I forgave a version of me that only knew how to brace—
how to tighten every muscle like the world was about to break.
I let my shoulders drop in the middle of a crowded room.
I let my stomach loose.
I laughed with my mouth wide open, even when it startled me.
I cried without a script for what I'd say after.

I let myself sleep in.
I let myself be late.
I let myself be loved in small, clumsy ways
and didn't question if I deserved it.

The softest thing I did this year was stay—
unpolished, unfinished,
here anyway.

Being real is a risk.
People will flatten you into versions that make sense.
They'll twist your softness into spectacle,
your silence into distance.
Let them.

You weren't built for comprehension —
you were built for depth.
And not everyone can swim that far.

Control was never real.
Only the fear of losing it.

Sweat It Out

Motion.
Dance.
Reclaim your body, your space.

Find joy in movement.
Lift your hands high above your head—
move where the wind may take you.
Let music find the places you forgot to touch.
Let rhythm undo the corners you've kept folded.

Stretch your ribs until they remember
how breath sounded
before it became survival.

Step into yourself again—
on your own.
No choreography, no mirror,
just skin and gravity
and a pulse that belongs only to you.

Take a moment with yourself
where you flail and twist and shout and exist,
because moments like this
do not ask permission to stay.

So sweat it out.
Let your pores release the promise
of being rigid

in a world that expects you to stay still.

Let your heartbeat rise like a drum.
Let your body find its way back to rhythm.
Let motion become mercy,
and sweat become proof that you were here.

You will feel the air again—
how it curls around your wrists,
how it slips down your spine like forgiveness.
You will hear your chest
catch and carry
the sound of its own freedom.

And when it's done—
when the room is quiet
and your breath is a tide against your teeth—
you'll understand it was never about dancing.

It was about remembering
that joy can live
in a body that once only knew ache.

This is not performance.
This is resurrection.
A release.
A reclamation.

To Let Guilt Rest

forgive yourself
for the things you did
when you didn't know better.

forgive yourself
for the ways you tried to matter
and called it love.

you are allowed to outgrow your guilt.
you are allowed to rest
without earning it.

look forward.
that's all that's left to do.
the past has already taken
more than its share of you.

forgive yourself
for the things you did
to survive
before you knew another way.

let guilt rest.
it's served its sentence.

Breath Still Caught Between Becoming

there are still parts of me that flinch
when kindness stays.

Still moments I forget
I am no longer waiting to be chosen.
some nights, I touch the outlines
of who I used to be—
the ache, the hunger,
the silence I once mistook for strength—
and I thank her for surviving long enough
to bring me here.

I am not healed.
I am healing.
I am not whole.
but I am here—
breath still caught between becoming,
and that, too,
is a kind of arrival.

A Body Made of Enough

I used to think holiness lived elsewhere—
in the sky,
in the mouths of people who spoke softer than me,
in the distance between who I was and who I wanted to be.

But lately,
I think maybe God has always been closer.
Maybe She's been here the whole time—
in the breath I almost forget to take,
in the laugh that breaks the silence,
in the way I still reach for light
after everything.

Maybe prayer was never meant to sound perfect.
Maybe it's just this—
the small, stubborn act of staying.

My body was not built for worship,
it *is* worship.
Every scar a psalm,
every bruise a hymn,
every heartbeat a *proof*.

I am not waiting to be saved.
I am already here.
Whole in ways no mirror could measure.
Soft, loud, human, holy.

If I was once a body made of almost,
today I am a body made of enough.

Acknowledgements

To my parents —
this is the hardest gratitude to put into words. There are too many versions
of me you carried, too many moments you held together so I could fall apart
safely. Thank you for giving me a life sturdy enough that I could step away
from it, question it, return to it, and ultimately write my way through it.
Nothing I make exists without you.

To the ones who held me through every version of myself —
thank you for staying, for listening, for loving me before I knew how to love
myself back.

To the friends who kept showing up —
even when I hid, even when I went quiet —
your loyalty stitched me together more times than you know.

To the women in my bloodline —
mothers, grandmothers, and all the unnamed ones behind us —
thank you for surviving what you did so I could sit here and write what I felt.

To the readers who found themselves in these pages —
you made this book possible. You turned my private ache into a shared
language, and I will never stop being grateful that you chose to listen.

Thank you to the hands that helped bring this book to life.
To Hamza El Alaoui, for formatting this book with such care and precision.
Thank you for helping me hold it together, both literally and figuratively.
And to everyone who believed in this before it had a spine —
your love lives between every line.

And lastly, to the girl I used to be —
I hope this feels like a hand reaching back for you. You were never almost.
You were always enough.

About the Author

Alexis Dakota never meant to write a poetry book. She just couldn't stop.
This is her debut collection, but she's been writing since she was a kid— in notebooks, in margins, in half-dreams.
She hopes this book makes you feel less alone in your ache.
When she's not writing, she's probably romanticizing everything or dancing barefoot in her childhood bedroom.

@alexisdakotawrites

www.ingramcontent.com/pod-product-compliance
Lightning Source LLC
Chambersburg PA
CBHW021531150726
47990CB00006B/2193